The Chicken Coop Scoop

Written by Helen Dineen

Illustrated by Stephen Stone

Collins

Flora is keen to be a reporter.

"I can do that," thinks Flora with glee.

She scoots off at speed.

Elspeth is scattering grain in the brown soil.

"This is not a scoop!" frowns Flora.

Bree is training. She hoists logs.

"This is not a scoop!" frowns Flora.

Splash! Blair is dripping wet.

"This is not a scoop!" frowns Flora, and her tail droops.

Flora trails back to the roost. She hears cracking in the corner.

It is not a chicken egg. A crowd starts to form and they point in alarm.

Can it be a monster egg? Flora is not afraid. She creeps up.

As the egg cracks, Elspeth, Blair and Bree agree to run.

Flora swoops in. She has now got her thrilling scoop!

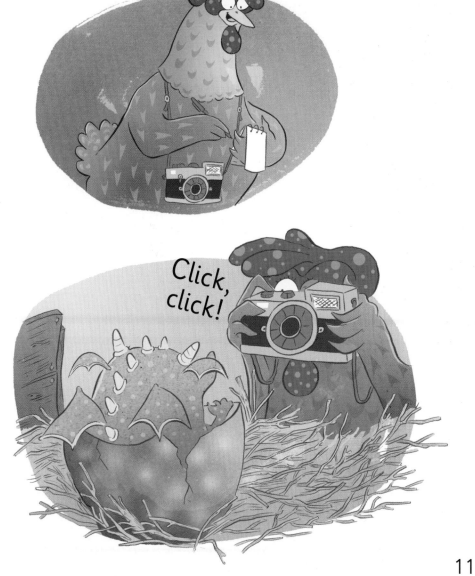

11

What a splendid scoop! Flora is the star of the roost.

Flora's dragon snap

But her stardom is short.

"Bad dragon," Flora groans. "You are a spoilsport!"

Map

After reading

Letters and Sounds: Phase 4

Word count: 169

Focus on adjacent consonants with long vowel phonemes, e.g. /s/c/oo/p/

Common exception words: of, to, the, I, are, she, we, be, you, they, do, what

Curriculum links: Science: Animals

National Curriculum learning objectives: Reading/word reading: apply phonic knowledge and skills as the route to decode words; read accurately by blending sounds in unfamiliar words containing GPCs that have been taught; read other words of more than one syllable that contain taught GPCs; read aloud accurately books that are consistent with their developing phonic knowledge; re-read books to build up their fluency and confidence in word reading; Reading/comprehension: link what they have read or hear read to their own experiences; discuss word meanings; discuss the significance of the title and events

Developing fluency

- Take turns to read alternate pages with your child. Model reading with fluency and expression.
- Ask your child to practise reading out the speech, using expression. Think about how Flora is feeling and how she would say the words.

Phonic practice

- Look through the book. What words can your child find with the adjacent consonants "st"? (*hoists, roost, starts, monster, star, stardom*)
- Can they think of items from around the home/school beginning with the following adjacent consonants? "fr", "dr", "tr", "bl", "sp", "fl", "st" (e.g. *fridge, drawer, tray, blinds, spoon, flower pot, stairs*)

Extending vocabulary

- Ask your child:
  - What does the word **splendid** on page 12 mean? (*something impressive or wonderful*)
  - How many other words can you think of that mean **splendid**? (e.g. *wonderful, marvellous, impressive, fabulous, great, brilliant, excellent, thrilling*)
  - Can you think of a sentence using the word **splendid**? (e.g. *the party was splendid*)